30 NUTELLA® recipes

Contents

This is an updated, sweet version of the classic club sandwich. Feel free to try different fruits, depending on the time of year.

NUTELLA® and fruit club sandwiches

MAKES 8 SANDWICHES • preparation time : 20 MIN

12 slices medium-sliced white bread • 8 strawberries • 1 nectarine • 1 kiwi • 1 banana • 160 g (generous ½ cup) NUTELLA®

1. Toast the bread on both sides.

2. Wash the strawberries and the nectarine. Hull the strawberries and cut into thin slices. Cut the nectarine into quarters and slice very thinly. Peel the kiwi and the banana, then cut into thin rounds.

3. Spread one side of each of four slices of toast with NUTELLA®. Divide half the sliced fruit between the NUTELLA® toasts, overlapping the slices of fruit.

4. Cover each of the four NUTELLA® toasts with another piece of toast. Spread these with more NUTELLA® and divide the remaining fruit between them, again overlapping the pieces of sliced fruit. Finish by covering each with another slice of toast. Cut each sandwich into two triangles. Secure with a cocktail stick/toothpick and serve immediately.

A teatime treat that children will go crazy for... These NUTELLA® palmiers will be gone in a single bite!

Mini coconut and NUTELLA®palmiers

MAKES 30 PALMIERS • preparation time : 5 MIN • cooking time : 15 MIN • chilling time : 30 MIN

230 g (8 oz) ready-rolled puff pastry • 150 g (½ cup) NUTELLA® • 15 g (3 tbsp) shredded coconut

1. Preheat the oven to 180°C (350°F/Gas 4).

2. Unroll the puff pastry and spread with NUTELLA®.

3. Roll one side of the pastry in towards the centre, then the other side so the two rolls meet in the middle.

4. Place in the freezer for 30 minutes to make it easier to cut.

5. Cut the rolled-up pastry into slices roughly ½ cm (¼ in) thick and place on a baking sheet covered with baking parchment.

6. Bake for 15 minutes. Halfway through baking, sprinkle the palmiers with the shredded coconut.

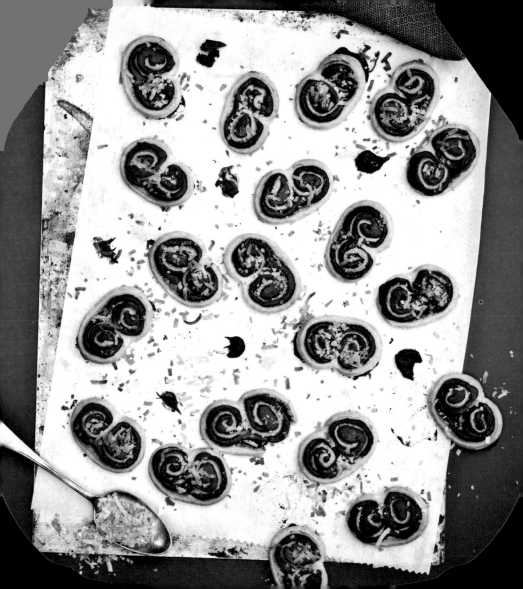

The combination of NUTELLA® and orange makes eating these little cakes complete bliss …

NUTELLA® and orange whoopie pies

MAKES 15 WHOOPIE PIES • preparation time : 30 MIN • cooking time : 10–15 MIN • chilling time : 1 HR

For the cream filling 1 orange • 75 g (5 tbsp) unsalted butter • 50 g (¼ cup) caster/superfine sugar • 1 egg • 75 g (⅓ cup) Philadelphia-style cheese
For the whoopie pies 125 g (1¼ cups) plain/all-purpose flour • 1 tsp baking powder • 40 g (3 tbsp) unsalted butter • 40 g (scant ¼ cup) caster/superfine sugar • 1 egg • 100 g (scant ½ cup) NUTELLA® • 20 g (2 tbsp) cocoa powder • 100 ml (scant ½ cup) semi-skimmed milk • a pinch of salt

1. Preheat the oven to 180°C (350°F/Gas 4).

2. Make the cream filling. Finely grate the orange zest and squeeze the juice. Melt the butter in a bain-marie or in a bowl over a pan of simmering water. Add the sugar, egg and the juice and zest of the orange. Beat continuously until the mixture thickens. Remove from the heat and leave to cool. Beat in the cheese then chill for 1 hour.

3. Make the whoopie pies. Mix together the flour, baking powder and salt. In a separate bowl, beat together the butter and sugar. Add the egg, NUTELLA®, cocoa powder and milk. Mix well then add the flour and baking powder mixture.

4. Place 30 small spoonfuls of the mixture on a baking sheet covered with baking parchment. Bake for 10–15 minutes. Remove from the oven, leave to cool on a cooling rack, then sandwich together with the cream filling.

There's a lovely surprise hiding in each of these little cakes –
a mouthful of melted NUTELLA®!

NUTELLA® financiers

MAKES 18 FINANCIERS • preparation time : 10 MIN • cooking time : 10–12 MIN

70 g (5 tbsp) unsalted butter • 50 g (½ cup) plain/all-purpose flour • 130 g (1 cup) icing/confectioner's sugar • 70 g (¾ cup) ground almonds • 4 egg whites • 50 g (¼ cup) NUTELLA®

1. Preheat the oven to 200°C (400°F/Gas 6).

2. Melt the butter in a small saucepan over a low heat. Set aside.

3. In a bowl, mix together the flour, icing/confectioner's sugar and ground almonds. Beat in the egg whites, one at a time, then add the melted butter. Mix well.

4. Grease 18 financier moulds or shallow bun tins then half-fill each section with cake mixture.

5. Add 1 tsp NUTELLA® to each then cover with the cake mixture. Bake for 10–12 minutes.

Lovers of coulants – those little cakes with a melt-in-the-middle centre – won't be disappointed by this perfect blend of coconut and that famous hazelnut chocolate spread.

NUTELLA® and coconut coulants

MAKES 4 COULANTS • preparation time : 20 MIN • cooking time : 15 MIN

140 g (1¾ cups) shredded coconut • 80 g (generous ½ cup) icing/confectioner's sugar • 40 g (2½ tbsp) unsalted butter, softened • 1 egg yolk • 100 g (scant ½ cup) creamed coconut • 3 egg whites • a pinch of salt • flour for dusting
• 4 tsp NUTELLA®

1. Preheat the oven to 180°C (350°F/Gas 4).

2. In a bowl, beat together the shredded coconut, icing sugar, softened butter, egg yolk and creamed coconut.

3. In another bowl, beat together the egg whites with the salt until they form stiff peaks, then gently fold into the coconut mixture.

4. Grease and flour 4 ramekins. Divide the mixture between the ramekins, place 1 tsp NUTELLA® in the middle of each and press it down into the mixture.

5. Bake for 15 minutes. Remove the coulants from the oven, leave to cool for 5 minutes then carefully unmould.

Tip: Press the NUTELLA® firmly into the mixture to prevent it from drying out and forming a crust on top when baked.

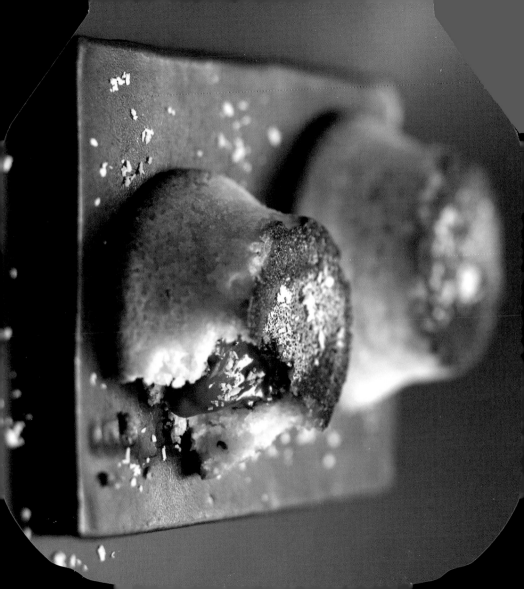

Banana and NUTELLA® tartlets

MAKES 6 TARTLETS • preparation time : 15 MIN • chilling time : 1 HR
• cooking time : 20 MIN

For the shortcrust pastry 180 g (¾ cup) unsalted butter • 2 pinches of salt
• 1 tbsp caster/superfine sugar • 2 egg yolks • 50 ml (scant ¼ cup) whole milk, at room temperature • 255 g (2½ cups) plain/all-purpose flour

3 bananas • 200 g (⅞ cup) NUTELLA® (approx 1 heaped tbsp per tartlet) • 2 tbsp macadamia nuts, toasted and chopped

1. Make the pastry. Cut the butter into small pieces. Blend with a spatula to soften. Add the salt, sugar, egg yolks and milk, and mix well to ensure all the ingredients are well blended. Gradually add the flour and knead it into the mixture by hand. Roll the pastry into a ball, wrap it in clingfilm/plastic wrap and refrigerate for 1 hour.

2. Preheat the oven to 200°C (400°F/Gas 6). Roll the pastry out on a floured work surface to a thickness of 3 mm (⅛ in). Grease six 10 cm (4 in) diameter tartlet pans. Cut the pastry into six rounds, each slightly larger than the diameter of the tartlet pans. Lay the pastry rounds in the tartlet pans and prick the bottom of the pastry several times with a fork. Bake for 10 minutes.

3. Cut the bananas into slices roughly 5 mm (¼ in) thick. Take the tartlet tins out of the oven. Spread the bottom of each tartlet with approximately 1 tbsp of NUTELLA®. Lay the banana slices on top and return to the oven for 10 minutes. Sprinkle the tarts with the chopped macadamia nuts and serve warm or cold.

A quick and easy dessert to make using the world-famous hazelnut chocolate spread; it will tickle the tastebuds of young and old alike!

NUTELLA® soufflés

MAKES 6 SOUFFLÉS • preparation time : 20 MIN • cooking time : 25–30 MIN

200 g (⅞ cup) NUTELLA® • 6 eggs • 40 g (¼ cup) cornflour/cornstarch • 120 g (⅔ cup) caster/superfine sugar • 1 heaped tsp vanilla sugar • 15 g (1 tbsp) unsalted butter • icing/confectioner's sugar, to decorate

1. Melt the NUTELLA® in a bain-marie or in a bowl over a pan of simmering water.

2. Break the eggs and separate the whites from the yolks. Sieve the cornflour/cornstarch into a bowl and mix with 60 g (⅓ cup) of the sugar.

3. Add the egg yolks, two at a time, to the melted NUTELLA®, followed by the vanilla sugar and finally the cornflour/cornstarch and sugar mixture.

4. Preheat the oven to 220°C (425°F/Gas 7). Beat the egg whites until they form stiff peaks then fold in 50 g (¼ cup) of the sugar. Carefully fold the beaten egg whites into the NUTELLA® mixture but do not work them together too much.

5. Grease 6 moulds or small soufflé dishes and dust with the remaining sugar. Pour the mixture into the dishes and bake for 25–30 minutes.

6. Remove from the oven, sprinkle the soufflés with icing/confectioner's sugar and serve.

Treat yourself at breakfast or teatime with these mini croissants made with the famous hazelnut chocolate spread!

Mini NUTELLA® croissants

MAKES 16 MINI CROISSANTS ● preparation time : 10 MIN ● cooking time : 20 MIN

230 g (8 oz) ready-rolled puff pastry ● 150 g (½ cup) NUTELLA® ● 1 egg yolk, to glaze

---

1. Preheat the oven to 180°C (350°F/Gas 4).

2. Unroll the pastry on the work surface. Spread with a thick layer of NUTELLA®.

3. Cut the pastry into 16 equal-sized pieces. Roll each piece onto itself, starting at a long edge in order to form a mini-croissant.

4. Brush with the egg yolk.

5. Bake for 20 minutes.

This may be a dessert that flies in the face of today's food trends, but it's sometimes good to give into temptation!

NUTELLA® mousse

MAKES 8 MOUSSES • preparation time : 15 MIN • chilling time : 6 HR MINIMUM

4 eggs + 2 egg whites • 2 tbsp caster/superfine sugar • 200 g (⅞ cup) NUTELLA® • 50 g (3½ tbsp) unsalted butter • 50 g (scant ½ cup) crème fraîche • 8 tbsp hazelnuts, toasted and chopped

1. Break the eggs and separate the whites from the yolks. Beat the yolks vigorously with the sugar until the mixture becomes pale and frothy.

2. Melt the NUTELLA® with the butter in a bain-marie or in a bowl over a pan of simmering water. Leave to cool. Add the melted NUTELLA® to the egg-yolk mixture then mix in the crème fraîche.

3. Beat the egg whites until they form stiff peaks. Using a spatula, gently fold the egg whites into the NUTELLA® mixture.

4. Cover the bottom of 8 small ramekins with a thin layer of toasted, chopped hazelnuts.

5. Divide the mousse between the ramekins and refrigerate for at least 6 hours.

Tip: For mousse with a firmer texture, place in the freezer for half an hour before serving.

To make a change from traditional crème brûlée, try adding a tiny touch of NUTELLA®. The result is delicious! Prepare the night before: the cream needs chilling for twelve hours.

NUTELLA® crème brûlée

MAKES 4 CRÈMES BRÛLÉES • preparation time : 15 MIN • cooking time : 1 HR
• chilling time : 12 HR MINIMUM

6 egg yolks • 75 g (generous ⅓ cup) caster/superfine sugar • 1 vanilla pod/bean
• 150 ml (⅔ cup) whole milk • 250 ml (1 cup) single/light cream • 160 g (generous ½ cup) NUTELLA® • 40 g (3 tbsp) demerara/turbinado sugar

1. Preheat the oven to 110°C (225°F/Gas ¼). Beat the egg yolks with the sugar until they become pale.

2. Split the vanilla pod/bean in half lengthwise, scrape out the seeds with the point of a knife and add them to the beaten egg yolks. Slowly add the milk and the cream, both at room temperature, and mix thoroughly until well combined.

3. Place 1 generous tablespoon of NUTELLA® – approximately 40 g – in the bottom of 4 shallow flameproof ramekins. Pour the vanilla cream on top. Place the ramekins on the middle shelf of the oven and bake for 1 hour.

4. Remove from the oven and leave to cool. Refrigerate for at least 12 hours. Just before serving, sprinkle with the demerara/turbinado sugar and caramelise the surface with a cook's blowtorch or place under the grill/broiler for 1 minute.

Tiny school-goers are sure to love this delicious NUTELLA®-flavoured milkshake!

Banana and NUTELLA® milkshake

MAKES 2 MILKSHAKES • preparation time : 10 MIN

2 bananas • 400 ml (1¾ cups) whole milk, chilled • 3 tbsp NUTELLA® • 1 tbsp caster/superfine sugar • 4 or 5 ice cubes

1. Peel and slice the bananas.

2. Blend the bananas for 1 minute with the chilled milk, NUTELLA®, sugar and ice cubes until the mixture is creamy and frothy.

3. Pour the milkshake into two glasses and serve immediately.

Variation: You can replace the ice cubes with two scoops of vanilla ice cream.

Add a little whipped cream to the top of these creamy desserts or sprinkle them with a few chopped, unsalted pistachios.

NUTELLA® creams

MAKES 8 CREAMS • preparation time : 20 MIN • cooking time : 10 MIN • chilling time : 4 HR

3 egg yolks • 25 g (2 tbsp) caster/superfine sugar • 250 ml (1 cup) whole milk • 125 ml (½ cup) single/light cream • 180 g (¾ cup) NUTELLA®

1. Beat the egg yolks with the sugar in a bowl until they are pale and frothy.

2. Bring the milk and cream to the boil in a saucepan. Pour this hot mixture onto the egg yolks, beating continuously. Return the mixture to the saucepan and cook over a medium heat, stirring continuously until the mixture just comes to the boil. Remove from the heat, leave to cool for 10 minutes, then gradually add the NUTELLA®, mixing it in thoroughly until it is well combined.

3. Pour the mixture into 8 individual moulds or 8 glass yoghurt pots, then refrigerate for at least 4 hours.

To make a change from traditional rice pudding, try this tasty gourmet variation!

NUTELLA® rice pudding

SERVES 4–6 • preparation time : 5 MIN • cooking time : 45 MIN

1 litre (4 cups) whole milk • 20 g (1½ tbsp) caster/superfine sugar • 1 vanilla pod/bean • 100 g (½ cup) pudding rice • 3 tbsp NUTELLA®

1. Bring the milk and sugar to the boil in a saucepan. Split the vanilla pod/bean in half lengthwise, scrape out the seeds with the point of a knife and add them to the boiling milk.

2. Pour the rice into the milk and cook over a gentle heat for appoximately 45 minutes. Stir from time to time to prevent the rice from sticking to the bottom of the saucepan.

3. Remove from the heat as soon as the rice is cooked. Immediately add the NUTELLA® and mix well to ensure it is well combined. Divide the mixture between 4–6 glasses and leave to cool, during which time the rice will absorb any excess liquid. Serve warm or cold.

To ring the changes, add a chocolate to the meringue along with the NUTELLA®, a little chestnut purée, or perhaps some salted butter caramel cream.

NUTELLA® meringues

MAKES APPROX 12 MERINGUES • preparation time : 20 MIN

• cooking time : 50 MIN–1 HR • drying time : OVERNIGHT

4 egg whites • 200 g (1 cup) caster/superfine sugar • 12 tsp NUTELLA®

1. Preheat the oven to 110°C (225°F/Gas ¼). To ensure even-sized meringues, draw ovals 10 cm (4 in) long by 7 cm (2¾ in) wide on a sheet of baking parchment. Turn the parchment over and place on a baking sheet.

2. Beat the egg whites in a bowl. When they start to become stiff, add the caster/superfine sugar, a little at a time. Continue to beat until all the sugar has been added and the meringue forms peaks when the beater is lifted out. If this does not happen, stand the bowl in a saucepan of hot water and beat for a few minutes more.

3. Fit a piping bag with a 10 mm (½ in) icing nozzle and fill with meringue. Pipe a little meringue in the centre of each marked oval. Add a teaspoon of NUTELLA® on top of each and cover with more meringue.

4. Bake for 20 minutes. Lower the temperature to 70°C (160°F) and cook for 30–40 minutes more.

5. Remove the meringues from the oven and leave to dry overnight before serving.

You can replace the gelatine in this recipe with agar-agar. If you plan to do this, use half a teaspoon of agar-agar to 400 ml (1¾ cups) cream.

NUTELLA® panna cotta

MAKES 4 PANNE COTTE • preparation time : 10 MIN • cooking time : 3 MIN
• chilling time : 3 HR MINIMUM

2 leaves of gelatine • 400 ml (1¾ cups) single/light cream • 160 g (generous ½ cup) NUTELLA®

---

1. Soften the gelatine in a small bowl of cold water.

2. Bring the cream to the boil in a saucepan. Add the NUTELLA® and mix with a spatula until well combined.

3. Squeeze the excess water from the gelatine and, away from the heat, add the gelatine to the NUTELLA® cream. Mix well.

4. Divide the panna cotta between four small glasses. Leave to cool then refrigerate for at least 3 hours.

Take some caramel and some NUTELLA®, and voilà – such delicious lollies that you'll wish you were a child again!

Caramel cream NUTELLA® lollies

MAKES 12 LOLLIES • preparation time : 40 MIN • cooking time : 2 MIN • chilling time : 30 MIN + 5 HR

70 g (⅓ cup) NUTELLA® • 110 g (3 oz) salted caramel cream (available from delicatessens)

1. Dissolve the NUTELLA® in a bain-marie or in a bowl over a pan of simmering water. Set half aside. Pour a thin layer of NUTELLA® in the bottom of 12 small round silicone moulds. Refrigerate for 30 minutes.

2. Place a hazelnut-sized piece of salted caramel cream in each mould and cover with the reserved NUTELLA®. Place an ice lolly stick in each lolly and refrigerate for approximately 5 hours more.

3. Twist the moulds to release the lollies. Serve immediately.

Mini Swiss rolls? Yes, but this time made with NUTELLA®!
Loved by all, but especially those who are still children at heart.

NUTELLA® mini swiss rolls

MAKES 4 MINI SWISS ROLLS • preparation time : 15 MIN • cooking time : 10–15 MIN

4 eggs • 120 g (⅔ cup) caster/superfine sugar • 40 g (⅓ cup) plain/all-purpose flour
• a pinch of salt • 200 g (⅞ cup) NUTELLA®
For the icing 50 g (2 oz) pâtissier's chocolate

1. Preheat the oven to 180°C (350°F/Gas 4). Break the eggs and separate the whites from the yolks. Beat the yolks vigorously with the sugar until the mixure becomes pale and frothy. Add the flour. In another bowl, beat the egg whites with a pinch of salt. Use a spatula to fold the whites carefully into the egg yolk and sugar mixture.

2. Pour the mixture onto a 40 x 30 cm (16 x 12 in) baking sheet covered with baking parchment. Bake for 10–15 minutes.

3. Remove from the oven. Immediately cut the sponge into 4 equal-sized pieces, but do not separate the pieces nor remove them from the baking parchment. Roll the sponge up in the parchment and leave to cool for a few minutes.

4. Unroll the sponge, remove the baking parchment and spread each of the 4 pieces with NUTELLA®. Roll each one up separately to form mini swiss rolls.

5. Cut the chocolate into small pieces and melt in a bain-marie or in a bowl over a pan of simmering water. Using the blade of a knife or a spatula, coat the mini swiss rolls with chocolate. Leave to harden at room temperature.

Your guests will be bowled over by this lovely cake. Sprinkle the top with milk-chocolate flakes and it will be even more tasty.

NUTELLA® and petit beurre cheesecake

SERVES 8–10 • preparation time : 15 MIN • cooking time : 1 HR + 30 MIN
• chilling time : 30 MIN + 12 HR

250 g (9 oz) petit beurre or other plain biscuits/cookies • 100 g (7 tbsp) unsalted butter • 50 g (2 oz) plain chocolate • 150 g (scant ½ cup) NUTELLA® • 200 ml (¾ cup) single/light cream • 600 g (2½ cups) Philadelphia-style cheese • 4 eggs

1. Preheat the oven to 150°C (300°F/Gas 2). Melt the butter in a bain-marie or in a bowl over a pan of simmering water.

2. Crumble the biscuits/cookies into a small bowl then add the melted butter. Mix well then place the mixture in a greased cake tin, preferably a loose-bottomed one. Press the biscuit/cookie crumbs down with, for example, the bottom of a glass. Refrigerate for at least 30 minutes.

3. Put the chocolate, NUTELLA® and cream in a saucepan and heat to dissolve. Mix well. In a separate bowl, beat together the cheese and the eggs then add the NUTELLA® mixture. Pour this mixture into the cake tin on top of the biscuit/cookie crumbs.

4. Bake for 60 minutes then turn off the oven. Leave the cheesecake in the oven for 30 minutes more. Remove from the oven and chill for at least 12 hours before serving.

A crumble to die for! Don't be afraid to use different fruits: bananas or apples go very well with NUTELLA® too! To make this dessert even more enticing, serve with vanilla ice cream.

Pear and NUTELLA® crumble

SERVES 4–6 • preparation time : 15 MIN • cooking time : 25 MIN

6 pears • 200 g (⅞ cup) NUTELLA® • 40 g (2½ tbsp) unsalted butter • 30 g (2½ tbsp) demerara/turbinado sugar • 60 g (⅔ cup) plain/all-purpose flour • 20 g (4 tbsp) ground almonds

1. Preheat the oven to 180°C (350°F/Gas 4). Wash and peel the pears then cut them into small cubes. Layer the pear cubes in the bottom of an ovenproof dish and, using the back of a tablespoon, spread them with NUTELLA®; if it is difficult to spread the NUTELLA®, place the jar in hot water for 2 or 3 minutes to make it more runny.

2. Cut the butter into small pieces. Place in a bowl with the demerara/turbinado sugar, flour and ground almonds. Work the ingredients together with your fingertips until the mixture resembles breadcrumbs.

3. Sprinkle this mixture on top of the NUTELLA® and bake for approximately 25 minutes; the crumble should be nicely golden. Serve warm.

This tart is traditionally eaten in France on Twelfth Night. Whoever finds the lucky charm or bean in his or her serving, becomes "king" and wears a paper crown.

NUTELLA® Twelfth Night tart

SERVES 8–10 • preparation time : 15 MIN • cooking time : 25 MIN

220 g (1 cup) NUTELLA® • 2 eggs + 1 egg yolk, to glaze • 120 g (scant 1½ cups) ground hazelnuts • 2 x 230 g (8 oz) ready-rolled puff pastry

1. Preheat the oven to 220°C (425°F/Gas 7). In a bowl, mix together the NUTELLA®, eggs and ground hazelnuts.

2. Unroll the first sheet of puff pastry onto a baking sheet covered with baking parchment. Using the back of a tablespoon, carefully spread the pastry with a layer of the NUTELLA® mixture. Leave a 1.5-cm (⅝-in) border for joining the two sheets of pastry together more easily. Place a lucky charm or dried broad/fava bean on top of the NUTELLA® mixture.

3. Unroll the second sheet of pastry and lay it on the first. Join the edges of the two sheets of pastry, pressing them together all around.

4. Brush the whole surface of the galette with egg yolk then use the point of a knife to decorate it with a large criss-cross pattern. Bake for 25 minutes.

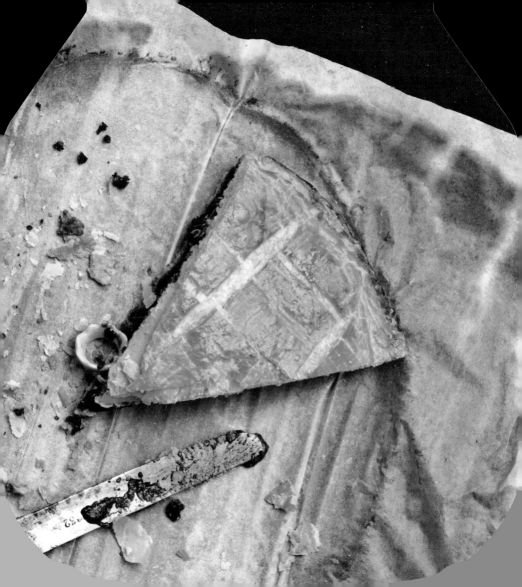

You can replace the bears with other decorations, but stick to marshmallow or the terrine will collapse under the weight.

NUTELLA® and chocolate terrine

SERVES 4–6 • preparation time : 1 HR • chilling time : 12 HR
• cooking time : 15 MIN

For the sponge 2 eggs • 60 g (⅓ cup) caster/superfine sugar • 30 g (⅓ cup) plain/all-purpose flour • 15 g (2 tbsp) cocoa powder
For the cream 100 g (3 oz) milk chocolate • 100 g (scant ½ cup) NUTELLA®
• 200 ml (¾ cup) whipping cream • scant ½ tsp agar-agar • 8 chocolate-covered marshmallow bears, or other chocolate-covered marshmallow shapes

1. Preheat the oven to 180°C (350°F/Gas 4). Using an electric mixer, beat the eggs and sugar together for 4 or 5 minutes. With a spatula, gently fold in the flour and sieved cocoa powder. Spread the mixture on a baking sheet covered with baking parchment. Bake for 15 minutes. Leave the sponge to cool on a damp tea/dish towel or on a clean sheet of baking parchment.

2. Melt the milk chocolate with the NUTELLA® in a bain-marie or in a bowl over a pan of simmering water. In a saucepan, bring 50 ml (3 tbsp) of the cream to the boil with the agar-agar. Away from the heat, add the chocolate mixture. Mix well then leave to cool. Beat the remaining cream until it forms stiff peaks then gently fold in the chocolate mixture.

3. Line a loaf tin with the marshmallow bears. Pour in the mixture then cover with a rectangle of the sponge cake, cut to fit the top of the tin. Refrigerate for 12 hours. Run hot water quickly over the outside of the tin then carefully turn the terrine out onto a serving dish. Serve well chilled.

You can really taste the NUTELLA® in this dessert! It is best to prepare the charlotte the night before: the longer it is chilled, the better it will hold its shape.

NUTELLA® charlotte

SERVES 4–6 • preparation time : 20 MIN • chilling time : 12 HR MINIMUM

500 ml (2 cups) whole milk • 4 tsp cocoa powder • 50 g (¼ cup) caster/superfine sugar • 275 g (10 oz) roses de Reims biscuits/cookies or sponge/ladies fingers • 250 ml (1 cup) whipping cream, very cold • 300 g (1⅓ cups) NUTELLA®

1. Gently heat half the milk. In a bowl, mix together the cocoa powder with the sugar and add the warm milk. Mix well then add the remaining milk. Quickly moisten the biscuits/cookies, one at a time, in the chocolate-flavoured milk. Use the biscuits/cookies to cover the bottom and sides of a charlotte mould, approximately 12–15 cm (5–6 in) in diameter. Press the biscuits/cookies firmly against each other so the charlotte holds its shape once it has been turned out.

2. Put the cream in a bowl and beat it well until it forms stiff peaks. Using a spatula, carefully fold in the NUTELLA®.

3. Pour the NUTELLA® mixture halfway up the sides of the mould then top with another layer of biscuits/cookies soaked in the chocolate-flavoured milk. Pour in the rest of the NUTELLA® mixture to the top of the mould. Cover with clingfilm/plastic wrap and refrigerate for at least 12 hours.

Tip: If desired, line the mould with clingfilm/plastic wrap to make it easier to turn out.

Quick and easy to make, these tasty little crunchy treats are perfect for any occasion.

NUTELLA® clusters

MAKES 15 CLUSTERS • preparation time : 10 MIN • cooking time : 5 MIN • chilling time : 2 HR

90 g (3 oz) milk chocolate • 120 g (scant ½ cup) NUTELLA® • 40 g (1¾ cups) cornflakes

1. Melt the chocolate and NUTELLA® in a saucepan over a gentle heat. When they are melted, add the cornflakes. Mix together carefully.

2. Put small mounds of the mixture on a sheet of baking parchment or in small paper cases. Chill for at least 2 hours before serving.

NUTELLA® macaroons

MAKES 40 SMALL MACAROONS • preparation time : 40 MIN • cooking time : 15 MIN
• resting time : 20 MIN • chilling time : 24 HR

6 egg whites • 260 g (2 cups) icing/confectioner's sugar • 240 g (2¾ cups) ground almonds • 30 g (¼ cup) cocoa powder • 200 g (1 cup) caster/superfine sugar • 400 g (1¾ cups) NUTELLA®

1. Preheat the oven to 140°C (275°F/Gas 1). Mix together the icing/confectioner's sugar, ground almonds and cocoa powder. Sieve the mixture finely.

2. Beat the egg whites in a bowl; when they are frothy, add half the caster/superfine sugar and continue to beat. When they start to become stiff, add the remaining sugar and continue beating to make a thick meringue mixture. Using a spatula, fold in the sieved ingredients. Use large, gentle movements for at least 2 minutes, working the mixture from the edges of the bowl towards the centre. The mixture should form a ribbon when it falls from a spoon.

3. Cover a baking sheet with baking parchment and draw evenly spaced 3.5 cm- (1½ in-) diameter circles on it. Pour the mixture into a piping bag fitted with a plain nozzle and pipe it onto the parchment in rounds the same diameter as the circles. Set aside for 20 minutes in a dry place until a crust forms on the surface.

4. Before putting the macaroons in the oven, place the baking sheet on top of another baking sheet: that way the bottom of the macaroons will not be overcooked. Bake for 15 minutes, leaving the door of the oven slightly ajar.

5. Leave the macaroons to cool for 5–10 minutes then remove from the baking sheet. When cold, spread half with NUTELLA® and sandwich together with the other halves. Refrigerate for 24 hours before serving so that the macaroons soften slightly.

These delicious NUTELLA®-flavoured tuiles are so quick to make that you won't be able to stop eating them!

NUTELLA® tuiles

MAKES 20 TUILES • preparation time : 25 MIN • cooking time : 6–10 MIN

50 g (⅓ cup) hazelnuts • 35 g (2½ tbsp) unsalted butter • 2 egg whites • 80 g (generous ⅓ cup) caster/superfine sugar • 30 g (⅓ cup) plain/all-purpose flour • 100 g (scant ½ cup) NUTELLA®

1. Preheat the oven to 160°C (325°F/Gas 3).

2. Sprinkle the hazelnuts on a baking sheet covered with baking parchment and bake for 15 minutes. Place the hazelnuts in a clean tea/dish towel and rub them together to remove the skins. Chop into small pieces.

3. Melt the butter in a saucepan over a low heat. Mix together the egg whites and sugar in a bowl, then add the sieved flour, NUTELLA® and melted butter.

4. Using a spoon, place small mounds of the mixture on a baking sheet covered with baking parchment and flatten them slightly into circles using the back of the spoon. Sprinkle with the chopped hazelnuts. Bake for 6–10 minutes, depending on their thickness.

5. Remove from the oven and quickly place each one in turn over a rolling pin or bottle. As they cool, they will take on the characteristic curved tuile shape.

These little spring rolls are ideal for teatime or a picnic. Ring the changes by replacing the mango with banana or pear.

Mango and NUTELLA® spring rolls

MAKES 10 SPRING ROLLS • preparation time : 15 MIN • cooking time : 10 MIN

5 sheets of filo/phyllo pastry • **100 g (scant ½ cup) NUTELLA®** • **1 mango** • **2 tbsp flaked/slivered almonds** • **25 g (1½ tbsp) unsalted butter, to glaze**

1. Peel the mango, detach the flesh from the stone and cut into small cubes. Toast the flaked/slivered almonds in a dry frying pan/skillet. Melt the butter in a bain-marie or in a bowl over a pan of simmering water.

2. Preheat the oven to 200°C (400°F/Gas 6). Cut the sheets of filo/phyllo pastry in half to form 10 rectangles. As you work, keep the sheets you are not using covered with a damp tea/dish towel to prevent them from drying out. Place a few cubes of mango in the middle of the long side of one rectangle, near the edge. Add 2 tsp NUTELLA® and a few flaked/slivered almonds. Roll up the spring roll halfway, then fold in the sides and continue rolling to the end of the rectangle. Prepare the other spring rolls in the same way.

3. Brush the spring rolls with the melted butter. Place on a baking sheet covered with baking parchment. Bake for 10 minutes; the spring rolls should be nicely golden. Serve warm or cold.

Bite into one of these truffles and what a surprise – a caramelised hazelnut in the centre!

NUTELLA® truffles

MAKES 15 TRUFFLES • preparation time : 20 MIN • cooking time : 5 MIN
• chilling time : 30 MIN

30 g (2 tbsp) caster/superfine sugar • 15 whole hazelnuts • 50 g (2 oz) plain chocolate • 150 g (½ cup) NUTELLA® • 2 tbsp single/light cream • 30 g (1 oz) hazelnuts, toasted and chopped

1. In a saucepan, dissolve the caster/superfine sugar with 2 tbsp water to make a caramel. When it is ready, add the hazelnuts and mix thoroughly. When the hazelnuts are well coated with caramel, place them on a sheet of baking parchment and leave to dry.

2. In a saucepan, melt the plain chocolate cut into pieces with the cream and NUTELLA®. Mix thoroughly until well combined then remove from the heat and leave to cool.

3. Use a teaspoon to scoop up a nut-sized piece of the chocolate mixture. Add a caramel-coated hazelnut and roll in the palm of your hand to form a small ball. Repeat until all the mixture has been used, then roll the balls in the toasted, chopped hazelnuts. Refrigerate for 30 minutes before serving.

You can add orange zest to the mixture if you like. The flavour of oranges works very well with NUTELLA®.

NUTELLA® cigars

MAKES 30 CIGARS • preparation time : 15 MIN • cooking time : 8 MIN
• chilling time : 2 HR

100 g (7 tbsp) unsalted butter, softened • 100 g (¾ cup) icing/confectioner's sugar
• 90 g (scant 1 cup) plain/all-purpose flour • 50 g (2 oz) egg white (2 or 3) • 150 g (½ cup) NUTELLA®

1. Using a spatula, vigorously beat the butter with the icing/confectioner's sugar in a bowl for 2 minutes. Add the flour, mix well, then add the egg whites, one at a time, until the mixture is smooth. Refrigerate for 2 hours.

2. Preheat the oven to 200°C (400°F/Gas 6). Using a tablespoon, place small amounts of the mixture on a baking sheet covered with baking parchment, then flatten slightly to make circles approximately 6 cm (2½ in) in diameter. Bake for 8 minutes. Remove from the oven, leave to cool for a few moments, then carefully peel away the baking parchment. Immediately roll each circle up into cigars and leave to harden.

3. Melt the NUTELLA® in a bain-marie or in a bowl over a pan of simmering water. Dip the end of each cigar in the NUTELLA® and place on a dish. Refrigerate for a few minutes until the NUTELLA® has hardened, then remove from the refrigerator and serve immediately.

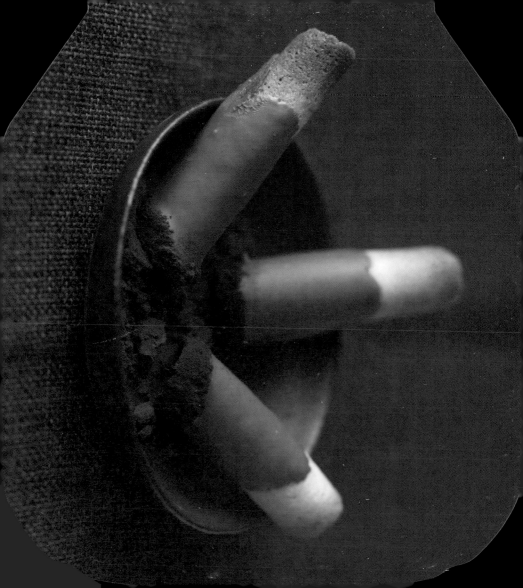

Try replacing the puffed rice with cornflakes or with some crunchy muesli.

NUTELLA® and white chocolate rice cakes

MAKES 25 RICE CAKES • preparation time : 30 MIN • cooking time : 5 MIN • chilling time : 2 HR

100 g (scant ½ cup) NUTELLA® • 80 g (2½ oz) white chocolate • 190 g (9 cups) puffed rice

1. Melt the NUTELLA® and the white chocolate in separate bowls in a bain-marie or in bowls over pans of simmering water.

2. Roughly break up the puffed rice between your fingers. Divide the rice equally between the bowls of melted NUTELLA® and melted chocolate. Leave to cool.

3. Spread the NUTELLA® and melted chocolate mixtures on baking sheets covered with baking parchment. Using a 3 cm- (1¼ in-) diameter biscuit/cookie cutter, cut into discs.

4. Place in the refrigerator for 2 hours to harden. Carefully remove from the baking parchment and store in an airtight container.

Kids will love these egg-shaped chocolate brownies!

NUTELLA® and chocolate brownie eggs

MAKES 4 BROWNIES • preparation time : 30 MIN • cooking time : 40 MIN

250 g (9 oz) milk chocolate • 6 eggs • 250 g (1⅓ cup) caster/superfine sugar • 2 heaped tsp vanilla sugar • 75 g (¾ cup) plain/all-purpose flour • 125 g (1½ cups) ground almonds • 1 vanilla pod/bean • 140 g (9½ tbsp) unsalted butter, softened • 250 g (1 cup) NUTELLA®

1. Preheat the oven to 150°C (300°F/Gas 2). Break the chocolate into pieces and melt it in a bain-marie or in a bowl over a pan of simmering water.

2. Mix the eggs with the two types of sugar but do not work them together too much. Fold in the flour and ground almonds. Split the vanilla pod/bean in half lengthwise and scrape the seeds onto the mixture with the point of a knife.

3. Add the butter to the melted chocolate and beat this into the egg, sugar and almond mixture.

4. Grease 8 half-egg silicone moulds, 10–12 cm (4–5 in) long, and pour in the mixture, taking care not to fill the moulds to the top. Bake for 40 minutes.

5. Carefully unmould the brownie eggs and leave to cool on a cooling rack. Use a knife to neaten the edges and spread the flat side of four of the eggs with the NUTELLA®. Assemble the whole eggs by sandwiching with the remaining four.

CONVERSION TABLE

WEIGHT

55 g	2 oz	200 g	7 oz	500 g	1 lb 2 oz
100 g	3 oz	250 g	9 oz	750 g	1 lb 10 oz
150 g	5 oz	300 g	11 oz	1 kg	2¼ lb

These conversions are correct to within a few grams (1 ounce actually equals 28 g).

VOLUME

250 ml	1 cup	3 cups
500 ml	2 cups	4 cups
	750 ml	
	1 litre	

To simplify measuring volume, here 1 cup is equivalent to 250 ml (1 cup actually equals 8 fl oz or 230 ml).

Publisher : Isabelle Jeuge-Maynart
Editorial director : Delphine Blétry
Editor : Johana Amsilli
Art Director : Emmanuel Chaspoul
Designer : Anna Bardon

Proofreader : Sylvie Ponté
Jacket design : Véronique Laporte
Production : Annie Botrel
Translator : Hilary Mandleberg

First published in Great Britain in 2013 by Jacqui Small LLP, 74–77 White Lion Street, London N1 9PF

First published in the USA in 2013

© Larousse 2011

ISBN 978-1-909342-16-3

10 9 8 7 6 5